Mystic Dreams

Hi Aunti Pegi,

Hope you enjoy this effort

Happy dreams

John Lawrence

Mystic Dreams

Lawrence Johns

To order additional copies of this book, contact:
Xlibris Corporation
1-800-618-969
www.xlibris.com.au
Orders@xlibris.com.au
500775

I dedicate this book to my devoted wife Kaye my inspiration.

Contents

The patient silence of the forest trees
Caress the glistening lake.
A cooling draught of evening breeze
Left calmness in its wake.

May I be part of wondrous things?
Or must one stand and dream?
I only know that my heart sings
Amidst those leaves of green.

Yet sometimes when my mind and thoughts
Surrender to the powers,
A gift that never can be bought
Is offered by the flowers.

A knowing absent mystic dream
Deposits in the heart.
Such heavenly magic peaceful scenes,
From such may we ne'er part.

The hands of time do not move on,
Nor can the I now fool.
All thoughts of mine are past and gone
Here only love may rule.

For love is all that can remain
When worldly deeds are done.
Here unity and love sustain,
Like radiance from the sun.

(Inspired whilst walking with Kaye around the lake.)

Nature at play

Watching a cobra through a window (in India)

Every day we watch them play
The monkeys and the squirrels.
They're leaping here and leaping there,
What lies beneath they do not care.
The chattering chorus alerts and warns
Of the dreadful reptile dangerous
Most of the day, Sri *Serpa* preys,
We watch him from the window,
His spreaded hood bodes not for good
For those too slow to see him.
Yet one small bird that has no fear,
Boldly attacks the hunter
Until Sri Serpa moves away.
Her children safe another day.

Spring Equinox

In leafy wood and quiet glen
Sweet blossoms now appear again.
Awake from pleasant winter sleep
Brock and squirrel new vigil keep.
The warming sun awoke red fox
Into a long day equinox.
The snow and rain and blistering gale,
No more such fauna will assail.
All devic hosts and fairy aid,
Rejoice within the ring new made.
Goblin and elf their part must play,
For spring, all nature must obey.
Flowered trees, fresh hollyhocks,
Prickly nettles, healing docks.
All will appear to change the scene,
Where only cold and snow had been.
To greened moor and grassy field,
All winter's terrors now must yield.
Whilst sparkling brooks among dark rocks,
Celebrate spring equinox.

The Karma of the Earth

In desert sands, if eyes could see
A forest great that used to be.
Where lizards live and snakes abound
Once there was life so full of sound.

Each hour each day the sands increase,
As forests fall and lives decrease.
No water left to give it life,
The deserts creep, the earth in strife.

What future for our children's sons,
When all we build is guns, more guns.
The youth today abandon love,
As men destroy the holy dove.

The earth, now hanging by a thread
Cannot supply man's daily bread.
Millions die for want of grain
Yet governments ignore the pain.

One hundred years a tree may grow
Sustaining air on earth to sow.
One man one tree a century
Providing life for all we see.

The karma of the earth we build,
Our universal debt unfilled.
The balance and the cosmic plan
Can we now stop what we began?

Spring Has Come

Now winter has begun its sleep
New seasons bright fresh schedules keep.
For now the joyous spring has come,
With life enriching warming sun.
Here parrots green and snowy white,
With pinks and grays reflect God's light.
Bandicoots with pointed snout,
Chase bobtail rabbits round about.
Flirty silver eyes so small
Dart around with chirping call.
Brown wattlebirds sweet nectar seek
That from the blossoming flowers seep.
High above in lofty trees—
Destructive white tails never cease.
Yet higher still in azure sky
The noble wedge tail eagles fly,
Searching o'er the earth below
For anything that dares to show.
Whilst we in awe, with great elation
Celebrate the Lord's creation.

How Far Away

How far away the dreams of man
To what we now have come.
How far away from God's pure love,
Such evils have been done.

How far away the ancient truth
Once taught from age to age.
How far away the holy word
Still guarded by the sage.

How far away that perfect light,
Now hidden by dark hordes.
How far away from selfish needs
The path that hate abhors.

Not very far if eyes could see
And, hearts were open wide.
Not very far the eternal flame
That in man doth reside.

For we are one, one perfect soul,
That nought on earth may alter.
One perfect love, such perfect love,
Can never ever falter.

Our God alone created man,
His image underlying.
Yet fragile frame cannot retain,
That, which is undying.

Deo Gratias

Bees abundant on blossoms white
Above clover, thick like carpets green;
Blue skies reflecting glorious light.
Small rodents run yet are not seen.
New buds now open to the sun
To show to all, what is to be.
The winters past the frost is done,
Spring now has set the dormant free.
All spirits lift on glorious morn
Faith in Creator's power exalted.
Expectant, on each brand new dawn;
There's nothing here that can be faulted.
Sweet bird song echoes through tall trees,
Then fills the earth with heavenly sounds.
This God-created harmony,
That in this perfect world abounds.
But yet, not only here, the 'one'
All through the universe extended;
A unity already done
Well known to him ascended.

So Happy the One

So happy the one who lives in the day,
Whose decisions are not marred by past gain
For there is nought that is gone
That should guide the way—
Or fill open hearts with disdain.
Just open your hands to the pure warming sun,
Let joyous sweet calm fill the day.
Each moment that shines, holds a new universe;
To know it will show us the way.
From the protection of 'I', one must surely refrain,
As into the unknown we emerge.
To be free from the known will enlighten our stay;
Face the sojourn on earth without pain.
(Then nothing but love will remain.)

I Dreamt of a Garden

I dreamt of a garden so pure and so grand
And in it, there lived every beast in the land.
Every nation on earth, red black, yellow, and white,
They all lived together and there was no slight.
No sun shone by day, nor bright moon by night.
Yet all were transfixed in a glorious light.
There were fathers and mothers all children of God,
No need for work or the turning of sod.
The food that they ate was a love so supreme;
It hung in the air and all were redeemed.
Walking amongst them the prophets of old,
The saints and the sages, with their message of gold.
Time did not exist, just a moment so fine;
No wanting, no needing, no feeling of mine.
On a hill high above on a carpet of green
The figure of Jesus could always be seen.
No parables told just a story so plain,
And all were absorbed without any pain.
So now when a doubt for the future of man;
Comes into my mind, I know there's a plan.
Now I patiently wait the call of the one
Who so loved his children he gave them his son

Splendid Scenes

Such splendid scenes we knew, now gone
Only in memories retained.
Such splendid scenes that were, now done,
Time, only ever can retain.
Views that fostered great emotion;
Create now sadness and despair.
Past sacred longing such devotion
Only our gods may with us share.
O men of power with hearts of stone,
You never linger long to see;
The morning dew or grass new mown;
Would you but set your spirit free.
Those forests great that greed has taken,
Could you but glimpse what others see.
Sweet memories then may reawaken,
To live again midst shades of green.
May false foundations soon be broken,
To once again build splendid scenes.
Then walk in peace through leaves and bracken;
Living such dreams that ere have been.

Fleeting Glimpses

This glorious earth well lit
By morning's radiant sun;
Displaying all that now must be
As he who wills befits.

Sweet heady perfumes gifted
Waft from blossoming trees;
Pervading wakening senses
To higher realms now lifted.

Encouraged here to understand
In mystic creation, man's humble part.
Foundations laid ere time began,
Obedient only to one command.

This *kali* age of mortal man
Confused illusion, locked in minds.
When newly stripped and rendered clean;
Reveal a love they cannot ken.

For surely, men will now come near
To 'that' which truly is.
Yet 'that' which ever was
May never be held dear.

To grasp and hold 'that' near
Shapes truth to melt away;
Then moonlight's cruel reflection
Will quickly reappear.

Harmony

All nature breathes in harmony,
Such shades of green now blending.
Still eyes perceive what ne'er can be
Conclusions false defending.
What is today tomorrow too,
Will never cause confusion.
That ever is, cannot be new
Compounding mind's illusion.
Conditioned thoughts depicting
To each a reason clear.
All clarity restricting,
Fostering naught but fear.
To be the universe anew
No senses now offending.
A gift when granted to a few
With great care, must be tended.
This omnipresent unity;
That brooks no slight division.
Declares a pure reality
And warrants no decision.

O Know This Man

O' know this, man, that life is death,
And so in death comes life.
To understand, this universal path
Sought, keeps the mind from strife.
Dark and confused the restless years
That o, so soon are gone.
Relentless cause of timeless fears
So brief and quickly done.
For what is truth? The question ran
Deciphered words, soon followed.
Those unrelated thoughts of man
Oft make the light more sullied.
Those sacred words that show the way
Hide layers of hidden wisdom.
Discovering one, dull minds do stay,
Their fleeting truths, depend on.
Then what is past, creates past dreams
Past ways of understanding;
Such sacred thoughts and holy schemes,
Will ever be demanding.

All Is One

When the muse upon us rests,
All thoughts of mine are stilled.
For we are here at his behest
With duties unfulfilled.
All life; that is on every plain
The love of God sustains.
His great breath flowing back and forth,
Like seasons wax and wane.
The glorious beauty of this world,
Brings tears unto our eyes.
Each undivided universe
All wisdoms, do belie.
Yet all again we must renew
When time demands its pay;
Remaining, til pure wisdom's light,
Demolishes new day.
Time then, will no more pain the heart
Burnt in the mystic fire;
For in this now, all now remains,
No doubts can ere aspire.
Man's subtle mind that grieves with hurt,
No longer will destroy;
A unity, this you and I,
That nothing can employ.

Thought, the Creator

From wretched thought, on crippled earth
Spring men of hate, and doubtful worth;
Such woeful cries of selfish need
Demand an unfulfilling greed.
All moral acts and righteous ways,
No more; without doubt are displayed.
Harsh melodies, and tunes now here;
Do foster and engender fear.
From men of God such anger shown—
To others shame, and of their own.
Our trembling world in mortal pain,
Her symmetry she must regain.

Prayer

How grateful then, we all must stay
To those, who meditate and pray;
Whether in solemn silence here,
Or in joyful chorus, loud and clear.
Those selfless ones of love and faith
Do counteract created wraith.
A harmony of sweet vibration;
Will gather in from every nation;
Joining in ever increased power,
To burst out in the final hour.
Then earth, her peace will soon acquire
All hatred burnt in cleansing fire.

Two Trees

The leafy pear sweet apricot together born
Never were two so comfortably laid;
Yet only in silence did they communicate—
Share and relate such wonders of life;
Roots entwined into ground, sustained,
Solid trunks alone, then grew, matured.
With arms outstretched, joined canopies of shade;
Self same earth, though different fruit;
Both sustaining fulfilling holy want.
Destined always to die, only to return, until,
That which sustains life is no more.
Then another will offer a new road home.

O Sad Vasse

(After seeing the state of the River Vasse in Bussleton)

How dank and dreary, o you sad Vasse;
That in past times naught could surpass.
In memory held by Noongar man;
Cherished land, pure flowing streams,
Glistening rivers held in dreams.
No need as now for cleansing plan.
Yet still a beauty is maintained,
And must be seen, in mind retained.
If then the mind remembering all
That those explorers first did see,
So rescued from an endless sea;
Their hearts and minds it did enthrall.
This all may see, St Mary's too
That England's faith they could pursue;
Lovingly built, by masons skilled.
Their moneyed masters needs completed,
Old parish temple homes repeated.
All spiritual needs, were here fulfilled.
Resting on those banks, in contemplation,
We hear the sounds of earlier nations.
The haunting sounds of songs long past;
Still from the ethers echo still;
Believing hearts to thrill and fill.
Great treasure held, their spells still cast.

After Bussleton

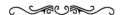

Parliament

So few the hearts in this parliament of men,
Can feel the pain of those oppressed;
Blind fools that see no wrong, distressed
Feel cleansed anew by daily amens.
One Lord one faith, one love of God;
The same not changed by powered command,
The same not changed by greed's demand.
Still, minds do turn to foreign sod
Yet foreign is from where we stand.
A belly filled, usurps mind's pain;
So cheaply bought for wanton gain.
To take a home, they hold a hand—
With promises to rebuild more grand;
Please, please they cry, please leave our land.

(In disgust at the actions of parliament.)

The Silent Gardener

Have you noticed the man who nurtures the flowers?
Have you noticed the love on each plant he bestows?
Each flower responds to his God-given powers;
Sharing blossoms of beauty the only way that he knows.
Our Lord in his wisdom selected with care,
A heart that seeks nothing; but that all may partake
In that fragrant display, with such joy he prepared.
God gave us this garden insights to awake.
Let us be like the man, in the garden so sweet,
One pointed to beauty, in our thoughts to create.
As, only the good in man's future we meet;
Then, to all of creation we must surely relate

India, February 2009

Lost in the Beauty

Lost in the beauty of love, here now;
When all that is, or was, does merge
Into that dream, that so fills, then, thou
o restless one; feel not the urge
To fall in contemplation of such a mystery;
For ever were the ways, in tune of history.
Hold fast, all in time will reveal itself,
If not to your eyes, so to another.
It matters not, seek then not pelf;
For all is one, each man, our brother.

2

Great trees made green to calm the soul;
Great skies of blue, his mantle shared;
If not a part, then not made whole,
No divine blessed music heard.
The beauty found is not of sight
Nor subtle mind or human might;
It lies within, in silence hid,
Within the breeze upon your cheek;
Or breath, that's laid on each eyelid.
It is the nothing that we seek

Where to Now

Where to now, when marked thought
Leads back to places been.
Embedded deep in memories bought
From others, mine not seen.
Now years have gone, ne'er to return;
No use to lament ways,
So many left in treasured urn,
In revered place displayed.
Now, look anew with eyes not veiled
Stand firm on wisdoms gained.
Do not yearn for seas unsailed,
Within made boundaries framed;
For in past times as surely now
Great truths have shown the way,
Enlightened thoughts that show us how,
Waste not the limited days.
Look close upon this universe
It holds the keys of heaven;
Let free the soul, let it immerse,
Expand, as if in leaven,
Enveloping yet growing still,
Until made borders fail;
For in this place there is no will
And all blest wisdoms pale.
All colors known, then merge at last,
One light that's all pervading;
Containing all, no shadows cast,
Absorbing doubts unshading.
Yet, yearn not this extended bliss
It will remain tomorrow;

The many mansions here exist,
In paradise long sought for.
when all thoughts, are gone and done,
Can 'that' enfold and fuse?
Still more, become and be the one,
To live, to be the muse;
Yet, still the muse does live within
A greater silent nothing;
Beyond the Buddhic realms, sought in
That wondrous, silent, nothing.
In silence reached, in silence bound
That wondrous silence found.

O Wild Restless Youth

Wild and restless youth
So lost, so careless, no dreams
To hold and nourish roots,
Nor weigh the strength of truth
For naught is as it seems.
Wild and restless youth
Non to guide or show the way
Toward a love, on which to rest
Nor seek a moral quest;
A place in comfort stay.
Wild and restless youth
The flowering weed that soothes,
Already confused thought;
From dubious sources bought;
No benefits yet proved.
Wild and restless youth
The glass soon feeds the ire,
Enhanced by needed pills,
That lead to endless ills;
And stokes the dimming fire.
Pained and restless youth
From here a leap is made
Into a darkened void;
From poppy fields destroyed,
All hope begins to fade.
Distressed yet hopeful youth
Look now inward, and return,
Retracing all steps made,
Escape, be not afraid
Great truths you can affirm.

From the Garden

A rake a hoe, 'neath flowered tree,
Old barrow filled with leaves and grass;
Some bread and cheese, good company,
The word then told of times gone past;
Of winters hard, and constant rains
Of scorching summers, browning grains.

Then each with some deliberation,
Recalls a perfect glorious spring,
Then autumn days that gave elation'
So each one soared on angel's wings.
A harvest time with crops to spare,
Great bounty all could freely share.

To mete a fruit, that nature gives
Without a thought of whence it came.
Such plenty here, that all may live;
No distinguished part or name.
The joy is in the bringing forth,
It feeds the happiness of worth.

In this mode, all time stands still,
The present moment that all yearn.
No troubled thought or painful ills,
A lesson given, from nature learnt.
Created plant, so to, the man,
A part, within the cosmic plan.

Once Again

Should we pursue, what gift is given?
What heights of fame expected.
So many years of true self hidden,
So many, many lives affected;
Then realize, and hold in store,
What we have often been before.

No memories here, to bring to mind
The reasons for such yearning.
For on this path, ne'er will we find,
Our way, our road, our turning;
It leads us on from breath to breath,
Until we reach again dark death.

Yet in this dream, cannot be true?
Must life uphold wants splendor?
Refresh, support, and then renew—
Repeated same agendas.
Vasanas brought from centuries past;
Can truth reveal itself at last?

Ode to a Bird

O tiny bird o highest twig
In winter's bareness shown;
No place to rest and hide away,
Yet still you sing alone.
Perched high on lofty throne.

You warbling one, who joy imparts
To all who linger there,
And hark, to clear melodious cries
That spring is in the air.
Such news with all to share.

Still call again, that sweetest song
In daily rituals knowing.
Ah! Now, repeated answers too,
Set tiniest hearts a glowing.
And dub duel songsters flowing.

Soon nature's work, in motion sets
New buds to open wide.
Then greened trees new foliage
Deep, gives each a place to hide;
Concealed together inside.

This, on and on, till seasons change
To next pure ordered sameness.
For all again repeats and dies
In long continued likeness.
Revealed in nature's fineness.

Hidden Worlds

Out strolling on a calm warm day
Among tall trees, in springs display;
All that could be heard within soft breeze
Was birdsong, calling out with ease.
Calling, calling, each to their own
To all the same, none here alone.

And lo, upon a tree long felled
Among that leafy dell, did meld
A golden lizard, in deep sleep
Whose care all nature spirits keep.
They guard against, those not in tune
With worlds unknown, to man immune.

I foolishly approached with care
Yet still, he seemed quite unaware
That I could see his mystic form;
And wished no harm, just peace and calm.
A dwarf like deer his companion fled;
The charm was gone, the spell was dead.

Without a glance, both disappeared,
Into a place, where naught is feared.
The guardian too was wished away;
In changed scenes he could not stay.
For I had given pure nature's mystery;
Into man's dark, and doubting history.

If nature deems again to share
That gift once more, my heart laid bare;
My mind and thoughts I must secure,
And shatter not a moment pure;
But witness all without division,
Within this world, all gifts are given.

A Moment in Time

How often weak and troubled minds
Recall past deeds, solace to find;
Afraid to lose its tenuous hold,
A new decision then unfolds.
Then, temporary reason clouds the way,
Old judgments dawn upon new day;
For what is past creates the scene,
We soon become, what we have been
So many, many, times before,
Still, passing through an endless door.
What now is thrust upon life's play,
Is tainted, altered, deemed to stay;
Until the pained and troubled mind
Without a thought, this day may find
A view, perceived, untainted, clear,
Then past persuasions disappear.
All minds so cleansed without restrain
May hear at last, mystic refrains.
From deep within the very soul,
A sound to witness and recall;
The great amen the sacred Om.
Then witness, knowing naught is gone,
This moment here, reveals unfolds
A sacred jewel more than gold.
No dogma ritual, holy pomp
Can cast aside man's holy want.
For those that know, will guide the way,
All precious gifts will with them stay;
Until the question loud and clear,
Is asked of all, who hold truth dear.

Pure wisdom's pearls, from swine denied.
For never can such beauty hide
Inside a heart so racked with pain,
For all that is, it will disdain.
A moment clear will never pass,
It is within man's future cast.
What is today tomorrow too,
Is waiting here for me and you.
All earthbound, still yet uncompleted,
Are but pure spirit, undefeated.
A part of his great wondrous plan,
The promised gift to mortal man.
There hides within this fragile frame,
A part of him, who gave us name.

The Noisy Night Bird

Noisy bird, your plaintive cry
Disturbs the silence of the night
With urgent stories of love's plight;
So, on and on, till morn's first sight.

Yet still, you do, on grey nights cease,
When clouds all lunar passions stay
Reawakened with enfolding day,
And warming sun gives new release.

What makes you warble through the night?
Can it be moonlight's sweet persuasion?
Or moonbeams lent, for such occasion,
To bathe and soothe you in its light?

Or is it that you cannot know,
That you call out in great confusion,
Into a nature set illusion.
And sing to a reflected glow?

White Daisies in Profusion

How true 't was said of Solomon's glory,
When gazing upon nature's story.
A pageant placed before my eyes
A sea of white, 'neath perfect skies;
Each petal, reaching toward pure light.
Yet, Still they close and sleep each night,
To once again like waiting throngs
Awake, with nectar, midst honeyed songs.
The murmur deep of insects swelling;
Such gifts of nature, all compelling.
And as I sit, aromas, sweet
Do fill my senses all complete.
Then blossoming trees of many hues,
Alert, and tell of nature's news,
That spring is come in finest clothes,
All flowers bedecked in gilded robes.
This constant movement, God created
To keep all minds, and hearts elated.
Then, full of joy, and endless wonder,
All doubting thoughts are cast asunder;
For in this moment, all is one.
Creation's awesome duty done.

How then, have I come to this?

Some three score and twenty years,
The body tires the memory falters;
And yet, a deep feeling, ever closer,
That, what was so long sought
Is close so close at hand waiting,
Sought occasionally with a passion,
More often; sadly in forgetfulness.
How quickly these past twenty years
Or more, rushed past, without a thought.
This momentum continuing till of late; when
suddenly, the perfect symmetry of this world,
Overcame all the senses, and thrust itself
Upon my very being the sacred geometry
Of this ordered universe, apparent now,
That so overwhelms human logic;
And yet remains a wonderful organised chaos,
allowing ever, for the blending of nature.
How many lifetimes utilised, to arrive at this
Precious moment, a moment previously glimpsed;
Experienced many times, rarely grasped
Or held onto how often the baser instincts
Of man were allowed to roam, freely at will.
No thought of inevitable reaction or consequence;
As a stone tossed into a lake, cause a rippled flow,
Each reaching the farthest shore, which till now
One may never have trod; every action instigated
Creating a joining of events, now, unstoppable

Let the memories sweet or sad reignite all senses,
Then, and only then, may 'that' be known, 'that',
Which was laid out even before time was created.
Time that in the true sense of being has no reality
Important only to man. For as long as happiness
Remains based upon that which is desired, rather than
being totally reliant upon that which is ultimately ordained;
Each tomorrow, will bring with it apprehension;
And an illogical fear of death. *Yama* waits for all,
Until we see him no more.

To an Elf

Do not draw close to mortal man,
The great queen Mab, with tearful eye
Once warned, long after time began;
When, both rejoiced 'neath open sky.
A pact then made, that each would share
Creation's gifts, with hearts laid bare.

Beneath, within full leafy bowers,
In pure clear air we voiced aloud
The glories of the sun and showers,
From *Surya's* warm benevolent clouds.
Crystal streams, full, flowed throughout;
Diaphanous sprite frolicked about.

In freedom rode we on the backs
Of dragonfly and tiniest bird;
On this sweet earth, we nothing lacked.
Man before Eden, had given word
That nought would change or mar the scene.
All would remain as it had been.

Then, in that garden godly pure,
Immortal man, did change the scene!
A broken pact, love could not endure;
No-thing could be as it had been.
For mortal man, had soiled the earth,
His word, his duty, had no worth.

Now, man in time, lives waiting death;
No more with nature can he run
With each, as with immortal breath;
Denying all who live as one.
Those wondrous gifts of nature's plan,
Now driven from earth by mortal man.

Yet there are some who still retain
The gift, to glimpse all as before,
Just for a moment, feel the pain
Created when man, closed the door.
They bide young elf, till time is done,
And all rejoin 'neath nature's sun.

New Eden, earth will soon embrace,
All worlds in harmony will sing.
A heavenly joy on nature's face,
Whilst pixie dance in fairy ring.
When time no more can rule or pain;
Their unity all beings regain.

John October, 2010

The Mystery

What is greater we cannot see,
This fills all life with mystery.
So much observed with naked eye
Cannot such mysteries untie.
What seems apparent to simple man;
Is oft disguised midst nature's plan.

A Salamander

A salamander, I once did see
Cavorting, dancing with such glee.
Igniting, *Agni* in such form;
Setting ablaze without much harm
All branches, bracken, laid before;
Heaped high, and ready made in store.
All ashes then returned to earth
To aid blest mother, in rebirth.
Then tiny seed will show the way,
For all of nature's pure display.
Warm sun and rain will nourish roots,
A base for heavenly golden fruits.

Reflections

Old George

It is said;
There is great joy in remembrance,
Perhaps a time in past memory held sacred
A movement in time, when each spirit was enhanced by the land.
That time for me, occurred some long years ago,
When, as a lad I labored with joy my hands in the soil
The earth my true friend, companions few
Yet strong and reliable, two or three to mention;
Country folk all, most older than I even so all were equal
The land was all they knew, or wished to know.
.

One old George, I remember him so well, reflective and dour,
He spoke with a dialect that could cut the very air,
A West Country drawl, a farmhand of yore;
Gnarled worn lumpy hands, often tender and sore,
Yet hands that did no man a wrong.
On his back an old khaki shirt tattered and worn,
A leather waistcoat buttons long gone;
On his grey head a weathered old hat, stained
And much faded by sun, wind, and rain.
Old Corduroy trousers, tied just below the knees
With used baling twine, brown boots
Softened over the years, a sight to bring a smile.
Each day at mid-morning break, George would draw
From his aging old shoulder bag, a bottle
Filled with cold tea, no sugar nor milk.
The same each day, in a square tea cloth was wrapped
Thick chunks of bread some cheese, a large
Spanish onion, which had been purchased, no doubt,

From an onion seller from Brittany,
Who carried long strings of juicy onions
Hanging from a bicycle, often so heavily laden
It could not be peddled, only pushed.
Old George, was difficult to understand,
For as he spoke his ill-fitting false teeth
Would wobble up and down, added to
His broad dialect, this left the listener
Somewhat puzzled, and often perplexed.
Yet for all this, his knowledge, of the land,
And indeed of all nature, was deep and profound.
A wisdom he offered freely to all, who cared to listen.
George usually worked in silence, focused intently
On the task before him, dirty old pipe hanging from his mouth,
Sometimes lit often not, his work a meditation.
George could lay a wild thorn hedge, with nothing
But a well used billhook, until it became an impenetrable
Barrier to both man and beast.
Wielding a hand scythe sharp as surgeon's scalpel and hooky stick cut from
the hedge,
George could turn a wilderness bank overgrown with wild nettle
Into a neat playing field like surface within hours;
Yet in a softer moment he would show you
The place where red fox had lain some minutes before;
Or quietly disclose a badger's set, I swear he could smell
These most illusive of animals from afar, he had
become at that moment, as one with nature.

We Thank You, Lord

O dearest holy Lord, we thank you
For thy glorious gift of love,
In such radiant perfection
Shown in Christ the holy dove.

Lo! A stable bare and simple,
Thou sweet messenger so fair;
Born to us through Holy Mary
As told by angels in the air.

Potentates with gifts of splendor,
Came to worship from afar,
Many miles the kings had travelled
Following God's heavenly star.

On their knees the three then entered
With gold, frankincense, and myrrh,
To the birthplace of the Saviour
Offering their gifts so rare.

A child now shining in God's glory,
Destined yet to die for man
And fulfill the prophet's story,
Completing our Creator's plan.

O dearest holy Lord, we thank you
On this glorious Christmas night,
For your precious gift of Jesus,
Our Lord of love and grace and might.

All in Tune

How soft the murmur of the breeze
Shaking, cooling waiting leaves
Gently weaving through each branch,
Whilst spirits of the forest dance,
Leaping high from twig to green,
No trace to know where they had been
Nor yet to know from whence they came;
No need to know or give them name.
Appearing just when mother grants
Each glorious morn they must enhance.
No predetermined duty laid,
In harmony the way is made.
When all vibration is in tune
Then man with nature must commune,
Nothing may stop or mar the way.
To merit hidden denizens stay.
All men of nature are a part
A unity kept within the heart.
Hidden deep the way unfolds,
Now wakened man may then behold
'That' until then in mystery saved.
His part, like blossoming flowers displayed.
To know to be a part of all,
If so revealed then must enthrall.

Renewal

In the unrelenting heat,
'Tis hard to keep the mind complete.
The flora and the fauna too,
Drop wilting waiting to renew.
This land so burnt by searing sun
Will resurrect when day is done.
With evening cool the earth awakes
Absorbing gifts of liquid, sates
The want of earlier planted seed,
With foresight for the daily need.
Yet still the flowering eucalypt,
Down deep, within the earth still sips
Pure gifts of moisture plenty,
From hidden streams that have no entry.
Still in and on those blossoms heady
The constant hum of insects ready.
The radiant sun, all natures friend
Its scorching rays, on earth descend.
Whilst we as mortals seek leafy shade,
Industrious insects never fade.
This gift of God that pollinates
We so depend for bounties fate.
Their work of love is constancy,
A beauty given for all to see.

Empty Churches

Empty churches, save for aged waiting
A call, straining for an inner sound.
Man and Mammon here debated,
New changed values here are found.
From wide pulpit, word expounding
Fresh ideas, same god still feted?
Is this new god, that man is founding;
Must I believe then, god man created?
In image of man, fresh gods now made
To fit the human plan designed;
Yet none will see the plan delayed.
And nowhere their Creator find.
My God is in the great amen,
Above below, found all around.
A Savior given to mortal man,
Pure 'Om' the word, the sacred sound;
Vibrating throughout all universe,
Chaotic harmony, all things bound
Together, sing his sacred verse;
Transferred to man through fragile mind.

Sacred Sounds

Does the wind then hear the lark?
The music of this Aeolian harp.
Drifting sounds so pure and light,
Sweet ecstasies of sheer delight—
Raising memories through the night.
We hear those overwhelming chords,
A glorious lilt bereft of words
Weeping, through spidery strings discover
Sweet miserere like no other;
So soft and clear, you hear them, brother?

The breeze that through each string awinds,
Does lift the heart and still the mind,
Awakes the soul, midst splendid scenes
A meaning given, to closed dreams:
That voice, upon no human leans.
Then in this moment, all is gone,
Yet still is heard its work is done,
To be recalled 'tis so ordained;
A perfect beauteous sound contained,
Within brief memories ingrained.

Eagles on High

Each day they appear in early evening,
High in the bright clear summer sky.
Two soaring together, weaving
Amongst angry Crows, that fly
Not too close, nor yet to high;

Avoiding the vice like grip of talons
Waiting, the unsuspecting prey.
Searching ever increasing heavens,
The ritual flows from day to day,
In joyful, mystic, magical, play.

Two lovers, movement each expects,
Wings near touching, wheeling cry.
The closeness, each the one protects;
Uplifting winds intensify
The joy of flight, through heavens high.

One to the other, each for the other,
Oblivious to human wants and fears.
Without care destined to discover,
A feathered breast of blood and tears,
When from the earth cruel man appears.

Now only one, majestic bird,
High in that endless azure sky,
Remains to guard the loving word;
uttering a single mournful cry,
Circling where her love doth lie.

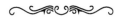

For Kaye

Memories of Middleton Beach

Scattered weeds bedeck white sands,
Broken shell from wave swept floor.
Misty rains on hills so grand
Sweep gently down across wide shore.
Seniors stroll on new mown turf,
Oblivious now to graying skies.
Supple young bodies ride white surf
Laughing, splashing, reaching high.
Folks in cafes ignoring drizzle.
Questioning bravely, how, where, why?
Ponderous of life's cruel riddle,
Still have no time for sweet reply.
Whilst you and I, contented muse
The play of life that is each day;
Sweet memories we may reuse,
Yet never wish to change the way.

Albany, February

Recluse and Solitude

(In a grove close by a river)

This I once found,
In one small grove of lofty trees
Long since planted, not by man
Rather by the whim of nature.
Did she so plan its beauty, its solitude?
For within the very centre, in the deepest shade
A fallen log, a resting place for the weary wanderer,
Lies in silent memory bound, such a place,
Where, the ill at ease, of mind or body
May find quiet and repose; here on a sunlit day
Sunbeams filter through the green canopy
Of leaves, caressing the stilled body, which,
With close eyes, absorbs the healing rays,
Penetrating, cleansing, repairing.
For what is man if not a part,
A part of this great wholeness, this universal
Unity, whose want, is ever to be in balance?
She seeks always to correct any disharmony,
Be it by her own cause or by man's pure folly.
It matters not, she sees no distinction,
Her Creator-given design must ever follow,
Obey, and reconstruct any imperfection.
No frame of time can mar or delay her work.
Experiencing this, could any sensing being
Deny their Creator or doubt their own place or worth?
For all must be one, on every plain.

In Melancholic Mood

A great conglomeration of pent-up anger
Now bursts, upon this indolent world,
Hatred filled rage—
Blind force of recompense
Demanded, instantly without hope

No place seen to turn or hide,
Forgetful of everything honorable,
Hatred fueled rage—
Blind force of ignorance
Demanded, instantly without care.

Waves of darkened days, envelope,
Draw down, waiting in cold rock.
Hatred filled rage—
Blind force of ages past
Demanding instantly, without compassion.

From north from south, east and west
Created energy explodes indifferently;
Hatred filled rage-
Blind force is gone,
Waiting once more, waiting, waiting,
Ever waiting.

Archangels

Those who guard celestial spheres
Great love is theirs to use.
Compassion gifted through the years;
In hope that man may fuse.

This heavenly council gifted down
Upon dark worlds of death
Do wait a recognitial sound
A joining of one breath.

They wait, until war ravaged worlds
Of man, and beast are soothed;
Then his pure glory will unfurl
When man is bathed in truth.

Limitation changed, illumination found,
Celestial sons of the most high
Their freedoms trumpets sound'
And fill a heavenly sky.

Awaken then the word of one
One undivided whole,
His greatest gift, the anointed one
Let still your heart enthrall.

The Old Camp Site

Through quiet woods we ambled
Between thinned, Jarrah trees.
Ruins covered now by bramble
Crumbled bases, still are seen,

Here youthful strength and eagerness
Was gathered, garnered in;
By faceless voices from far west,
So sure, so free from sin.

From fen and field, the call was sung,
By many, not yet men.
They rushed toward the sound of gun
The final great, amen.

Vociferous voices still maintained
They echo through the night,
A ghostly sound impressed retained
A timeless, sacred light.

Yet some do call from foreign coil,
From lands they knew not then;
They rest beneath another's soil,
Eternal friendships blend;

They call with mystic warning cry,
To brothers undiscerned;
Beneath a fresh created sky
Destined never to return.

New voices added to the throng,
Within the ruins stirring,
'Tis where the spirits play their song
Together, comrades yearning.

Still they call, the faceless herd
To innocent, eager youth.
Young men manipulated by a word,
A sacrifice for truth?

Dreams and Memories

Can mere words describe the dreams,
The wonders drifting through the mind;
Sweet places known, we have not been;
Our waking thoughts may never find,
The beauties we have left behind.

Then sometimes faces, we have known,
Of those no longer here at hand
Appear, to greet us, and renew
Old memories buried in sacred land,
That resurrect at their command.

Do they then call, lest we forget
The pleasant moments that we shared;
Assure us then of no regret,
And keep us ever, so prepared
For what is thought, yet never dared

O, what of that pure heavenly choir
Celestial music of night's hours,
It haunts, its beauty never tires,
An energy the mind empowers;
Angelic voices, blossoming flowers.

So through the day in contemplation,
A glimpse of night's reality dawns;
A mind in fragile meditation
Allows past faith to be reborn;
Then eagerly awaits new morn.

Printed in Australia
250363AU00002B/1/P

9 781462 876723